THE REDCOATS

THE REDCOATS

RYAN MURPHY

KRUPSKAYA • 2010

for Kira

ACKNOWLEDGEMENTS

I would like to thank the editors of the publications in which some of these poems first appeared: *Carve, The Canary, Effing Magazine, Fence, Harp & Altar, OR, The Paris Review, The Portable Boog Reader, Provincetown Arts, RealPoetik, The Recorder, Spinning Jenny, TIGHT, Unsaid,* and *Zoland Poetry.*

"Summer, Thunder" was first published by Big Game Books.

"Poems for the American Revolution" was published as a chapbook of the same name by the Dutchess County Department of Occupational Training.

Cover Design: Frank Mueller
Book Design: Wayne Smith

Distibuted by Small Press Distribution, Berekley, CA
www.spdbooks.org
ISBN 978-1-928650-30-0

K R U P S K A Y A
PO Box 420249
San Francisco CA
94142-0249
www.krupskyabooks.com

TABLE OF CONTENTS

"whisper in my ear
you're my pamphleteer"

— Scott Pierce

ONE

ANTHEM

Marsh under snow,
the sea spits glass—

salt-white in the glare.
A battleship cemented

to the harbor floor,
rust red at the waterline.

We do not halve.
Whose face in the spokes

of light?

It is a great comfort,
because you are not yet sleeping,

when the cat reaches out
to touch your face.

Sorry, I am not
communicating well.

Fainting is a *kind*
of swooning

sodden with, etc., etc.

Sudden and clearly
a night sky, the sea

spits stars.

THE GALES

Calmly Calamity dream in waves
Motion offense, local lighthouse, whose bulb we tend
Once at the corner of Remington and Colt
The N train through an arbor of I-beams.
The air a frenzy of pollen
A cumulative effect like narrative.
May its dark song lullaby
Shoulders out dark
unspool spring leaves
foundered forward

Oona is my daughter's name.
We spelt "cradle" without arms thus.
The Gales, or, the heart fails.
We discipline and sorrow
for example
I can drink and drink
and don't get strange.
Glug, glug.
Brushing, she bruised her wonderful hair.

Blushing, her goldenrod hair.
Capstan kiss, calamity
are the lighthouse days.
Blow the old man down.

Mercury confection the ebb
with abide, armistice,
Glug, glug
Ocean is my daughter's name.

Skiff in a field
pierced by the star
of autumn goldenrod.
Two days without sleep bleaker than sunrise suddenly pales
to see, to wake, to sad,
Gone in the lightning-rod days.

PRIVATEER

A stain what hearts last
Saddles a river through snow
In falling sunlight.

Eating an orange
Reminds us tomorrow is another day.

The general fog of the metropolitan
Night sky is warm orange—
And thus not alone.

Ain't no lighthouse
In that eye's dilated star.

A savagery sw-
Hollows me up.

NARCISSUS

Wind through our arms
Our entire putting on,
Putting up, putting together

Borne outbound
Service changes
The mirror, sickle-pale

In the rose of the river
lies another river
Sickle-pale

We wind
through our arms

Hum to the machine
knotted in our throat

Peering over the gunwale
To swallow his reflection

COURSE

Silts in, storms back. Shy volts
of the lily-eyed.
Every word has been for you
a beacon
lights beyond the breakwater.
A sun has built its nest in the boughs.
Their bleached calligraphy—

You are near me.

Hornets, black sails, the flight of cranes.
I can't sleep.
Like a tongue in its bell,
every "you" is faithful
to someone,
though you alone will know it.
As water too (or how it went)
overflows its element.

RINGTIDE

Ambien, ringtide
black with rigging
Is sun in February, snowvolt
stunned to stillness with impending

To sit and wait is terrible.
Dumb is the ocean
Fucker

Combustible practices, to say nothing
of the birds in the fields,
the Rent-Stabilization Act of nineteen seventy something.

The bottom bottoms out
a fury. I'm thirty
I should be better by now.

Is three thousand dollars famous?
Just so you know.
If there is wreck in me

THE WRECK OF THE *MARIE CLARE*

Lungs expand to strain their staves.
O concertina.
Today the cap is off the toothpaste
Begun, like winter, in earnest.
I do not mind to

suffering

the fog in the trees, the harbor, the fog
is in my heart.
A rattle in my chest I mean
to cough

You see, we are not so proud as to seem baffled
As a thread, unfurls, spirals floorward.
Radiator feedback leaches color.
A neighbor runs scales on the violin like a voice,

like a cavity. Floodlights define the dark like glower
Knots fall apart in your fingers. It caves
of bright

SPILLWAY

I haven't been out all day.
Orion—
The wind fleured. Spills in
the lees.
And the rain falls exactly
like rain only inside you.

TWO

SEA LEVEL

1.

Socket violence
bludgeon to begin.

Dry leaves rattle in a wind's
eddy perfect

October sprawls
from horizon to

horizon.
From which the hence
of anxiety broke.

I will burn all of my shirts.

You begin to prose.
Disloyal quiet as misread
when twilit

its own fortune

2.

Morning comes
in its big white hearse.

Then sudden and sour,

salt-glass and respite
and offer or regret.

Together we unspool
the cassette

with our fingers
on the bed

and sit in that shiny
black sound.

HARTFORD

In the age of butterscotch
we waited
for the lamps to come on
and on at any moment

Don't leave me
to fend for myself.

With effort we could slant
our own noon. Or,
that this feeling
is autumn and
not Hartford

Hartford, whatever you are,
don't ever change.

No, we are bleak
drawing closer.
Clatter soft-green
to surface

Flowering and flowering into

HELSINKI

Whitewashed September
and the Morse of porch lights—
I inarticulate you.
Wheel of sky in a birch grove,

all promise and exuberance.
I am gagging sometimes
too on the future.
Tropical storms on a weather map,

Marconi on the Metro
dark as the Finnish
sun. You are my last best hope
Charles Lindbergh, Amelia Earhart.

AWAIT A WINDFALL

Try to mean differently,

and not throw up.

Sun spindles to its last

in the rusting hulk of sky,

stars sick as knives.

We are bound together

by their vague threats,

kindnesses,

teeth like sleeping dogs.

Or I pistil in heat, is summer sleep.

Bludgeon and unspool

Thunder-cloth like bad weather,

portent,

whistles up

THE REDCOATS

Benedict of our small freight
lights athwart

The Haverstraw gypsum mills
chorusing

and our hammers
harbor Whitehall

the wetblack winter birch

UNTITLED

after Vija Celmins

White flowers trumpet from the night sky
Spinnaker of stars, threads of horns
Who we may know,
At most, only vaguely
Of.

Broken flowers of the bank machines
That light the sky
And you and you and you.

No, we are not alone
In the steeples of the night
And the vertigo of the theater catwalks
Will these days go on and
On? Is it dire to not think
So?

The pale green of leaves strata'd like clouds
Sing into the tropics of evening.
White flowers tourniquet from the night sky

POEMS FOR THE AMERICAN REVOLUTION

Revere

Bombardier, you laid the tracks
For our hundreds of eyes
Spine for flowers, spit azalea

The lush lawn of the vacant girls' school
Tuesday is Sunday only
No one is dreaming

Bunker Hill, I-95, the harbor subs
Like the face of a watch.
I should like to wake you, minute by minute

Clatter through the restless green night.
Bombardier, with your lantern eyes
And lantern head

If
If if
And by sea.

Knowlton's Rangers

Frail and dappled creature
Light like spilt milk
Not unlovely, silver buttons for eyes

Foolish to think I have a life
Other than this one:
Mottled, cascading floorward

The days are vast and expand blackly
Humid and aloof
Reverses rain
Independence Day, come what may
Stupid lotsa
                    shiftless red blossoms

Ethan Allen & the Green Mountain Boys

"Where a goat can go, a man can go,
where a man can go, he can drag a gun"
　　　—Major-General William Phillips at Mt. Defiance

Is it not enough to be loved
and repulsed?

Fenway—in your ashes
build a republic.

Silver battalions in green fog.

Sebastian, not a name
one should chose for oneself. Nameless
above Ticonderoga.

Lake Champlain
into the vowel of your open mouth
the water rushes in

The Kentish Guard's Fife and Drum Corps

After the fire truck's slow parade
—Otha Turner!
I have nicked my thumbnail
with a razor blade.

A wound bored its small daisy
into your shirt.

My dear wretch
we are ashuttle with flames.
And the dew of fever.

Little raindrops from your fingertips,
are you bleeding?
Poinsettia—

The Delaware, Champlain
Valley Tour.

That is not straw it is my hair.

Betsy Ross

Will we wake with July
inside us?
And if the stars are all hollow in our mouths?
Cornucopia.

The quiet building in my veins.
A building quiet starts in my veins.

Acela, splinter spires, Mass Pike.
I don't care what they told you,
a stone is not the flower of winter.

O Delaware,
dear George.

Red ears
blue lips
splinters for kisses.

Commodore John Barry

Speed the day.
Yes, the streets are full of threats
and children,
money managers and movie stars.
Singing in the wires.

And there is a feeling of fall
and summer and winter
(the wind from the west
off the river—
starry blight
persuasions)

And it is inside you
on certain days, when the light
is right.
And it is falling asleep,
and it is beside you.
Sleep the color of ashes.

3:17 am and the nightpilots
return with their charges.

A VALENTINE

We emblems
flicker

in this, the gray
lilac of February.

Hearts is ash.

Warm drone
from the amber

of medicine bottles.

SUMMER, THUNDER

No comfort
say the pigeons in the nightswell

The missing
head for the Brooklyn Bridge
No crashing valentines—

Give the ladies carnations and let them
run the bases
Crashing of church bells, the train
whistle skipping its stop

We take for this painfully
a pill
Dear, whatever happens
I can wake up from

The day
As ferment stains the sky
suddenly darkening afternoon

No crashing pigeons
The small birds cry out to be eaten by the fox and marmot
No thistle of blush

Rabid to dress down
in fitful British summer.

THREE

AUTUMN IS FOR BELLS

Autumn is for bells
And sagging ceiling plaster.

Oars plough wake:
Warn and victim we.

I am afraid to die
But RJ Reynolds whispers I'm not
And dying I believe him.

This is not the same as weeping for a cat's mortality.

Dear   ,

I would like to tell you that making people from words is not the act
of a tubercular child in an attic with construction paper. Worth and
companionship. Is not lonely. That they are more than parts of speech. My
friends might say otherwise, but fuck them, what do they know. That it is,
and has been, worth it I would like to tell you. I wrote and wrote and the
words began to fall off.

Dear   ,

The benches for the infirm and insane. I watch for a flash of pink on
Broadway, what you wore when you left, but the men on the benches zip
their jackets to their chins, read paperbacks through stacked pairs of glasses. I
thought you would pass on your way north. Or I chose the wrong route, the
wrong time, the wrong day.

Blooms early this city
And we are like that.

Leaves black in the sun.

This is the hieroglyph of the sheets in my skin upon waking.
And thus I wrote this to you in the dark.

Dear   ,

It's true, the spokes of a wheel only appear that way when they're spinning.
Commuter trains are terrible in every way. We name the stations for our
friends, or our friends for the stations—I forget which, it doesn't matter
now—it is better living on a real island now. Geographically speaking. Since
it has always been this way anyway. Is it more important to be remembered
right, or to see the flames lick the gunwales? Is it always the perspective of
the mourning? I never said these things:

That boy is dead.
And who is left to write letters to?

The rain that makes your hair grow.

FOUR

THE NEW MELANCHOLY

I've had to make my own dark
a year a day
Our tissue box shoes
our disrepair
Trees voice the wind
You dear municipal uniforms
you failed economic theories
Rep tie, knee socks, two hours later
and the storm streets now steaming
Brooch, broach, Copenhagen
in ice green

I dreamt again of batteries
In your chemise winding
the cuckoo clock
this figment green cuckold:
Come with your ghastly bouquet

RADIO SUN

If I could pare
and drought
the ever expanding
of winter.

To feel whole
against the
breath shattered
night sparking.

We've brokered
this peace before:
locate yourself
in the path
of abundance.

Come alarmist
cannon-fodder
tassel in your tricorner.

THAT YOU MAY ONCE AGAIN HEAR THE BELLS OF SEPTEMBER

In the sun's harbor
psalm rooftops quietly
Yes, they fill your arms
with light, cold reason,
the orange of Baltimore.
Damp. Lurid. June. 30.

There is missing as reflected.
Water-wound scores
you in your come-hither
you in your comeuppance.

Gone, the hippodrome of old,
is that nostalgia?
I will take you leaf by
Ireland, combing rupture
from the sandy bottom.

Tomo Ohka sadly
The chipped teeth in our
gear-head.
The hippodrome no more,
boys and girls in the park gazing skyward
tick tick tick calypso

ELEGIAC

Sunset, a grainy photograph,
night is lit
by a small black light.

As a child I would cry
at the sound of katydids.
Turbines of fear. The heart
has several gears.

We compass on the grass.
Two dreams there were,
elegiac and orange.
Your love is like that.

CODA FOR DOCK ELLIS

Said what you dark
grew back,

Larkspur, bonespur,
I can hear my heart

through the bedsprings.

What imperfections of light
in the orchard of your eyes.

What filaments, seams,
tenuous and thorn.

LAMENT FOR KIRA

Here there is suddenly

a dull metallic bird,

instead of sleep—

"A tunnel lights my table."

Listen, I feel this way

all the time.

Was beginning to forget—

The patient hand unraveled.

Sickness of molasses—What

Have I been hiding all along.

A future indicated

With limited sarcasm.

THE ONE IN WHICH JOHN GLENN RECALLS HIS YOUTH

Stomach ache, tooth ache, two
beers in the afternoon. Year
of the blackout. O young mothers.

A little color-blind flecked gray
goes brown goes red.
You know, like the old song says.

Affront. Mars. Constancy.
Congressional medal of honor.
A lawn chair festooned with balloons.

O sailor,
hove to in the orange night sky
through a spread of plane leaves:
cormorant, Mars, atomic.

TRIMMINGS

Grouse the lawn, fern,
dandelion. Slipping
insular. Stem systemic.

I am trying to stay alert.
She is the lawn dart
in my heart.

Now I've ruined it.

That we cannot lose ourselves
entirely in the world—
nor shut it
entirely
out.

Cannonball. And swift devout.

DELTA

When the veins of your sleep
delta and I am in doubt
or under an apple tree in rain,
purple roses from your forehead.

Robins, sparrows, the little scamps.
How shall we describe them?
We shall describe them.
It's all over-
rehearsed anyhow.

You've wanted to understand
me the way I've never understood myself.
We should have practiced
a difficulty—
and then. And then.

DUSK

Already the butterflies yellow with August
And the Jersey shore piled with houses
There are train whistles in the distance

Lonesome as the color of your hair
Unbound at sundown

From a window where
The light failed to your reflection

Silt of seeing—like a lip's blight
The lamps in the park softly
Come on

SPLICE

Mine eyes
and fading

fronds of light
that gleam

a match in
rain.

Clotheslines, a tangle
of pirated cable,

connect
our courtyard.

Some orphans maybe.

FIVE

THE RACE FOR MAYOR IS HEATING UP

I know this is not the hoped for
vacancy,
purple loosestrife gorgeous invades
the wetlands. Still collapsing.
And it's static like that,
somewhere burning,
streetlights canker the park night.

It's Bastille Day in Baltimore,
O Ativan
Too much trembles in the limbs
we ricket to small song.

The question of your hip,
and that burr of unreasonable hope
Yes, we built them, these stages

of nakedness
Marco!
Let them constellate in their swath,
Polo.
To the phlox of summer,
swan-dive, orange rind.

FIFTY STARS

To expect otherwise
in panicsoftly
corrosive—is to form dissent
Stanchion I pilloried to candidate the heartfelt:
"It's hopeless, Spartacus."
We are each on our own at least in this.
And, flowering in the still pond, concentric ripples
like secrets, gather and unique.
Meanwhile the tin sound of rain flecked with disappointment,
as the train exits the dark tunnel into the dark air.
From the catalogue of commemorative quarters: a very small owl,
an ivory tree, limb piercing a teapot,
a snowflake for her face (or some other constellation).

I have cannibalized other moments to invent this one.
Please retain this receipt for tax purposes.
Swanpiling   Steeplewedge
You flowers of autumn, you churning
plow, you archaic lamps.

ALL SAINTS

1.

I can't stop thinking of the nothing I want.
Five past eleven on a Monday.
Which is also awful.

Like sun through the smokelight,
or a phantom limb,
her hair a kind of feathers.

Visibly shaken. Heat scales
an advent of August.

More rope.

Or we can ballantine,
bask me in your light
of shipwreck:
stipple and shell and shall.

I mean, how often
can one remember one's posture?

2.

St. Brendan, you heartstar,
you graygreen spire,
I can't stop thinking of the nothing I want
to do.

This is how things appear
from the celebration of the bicentennial.
And the rigging over Rose Wharf.

I don't want to seem intrepid
sailor, we are friendless one and all.

O privateer, whistling in the courtyard
birds, sunflower and candles.

3.

Like sun through the smokelight,
the game called on account of fog.
Children with popsicle
hands waving in the fog horns.

The body, strung vibrant
with rigging,

daisystar, ark on a hilltop,
Spanish lights in suburban
backyards.

Bundle and squirm
we came with cacophony,
the light of shipwreck.

4.

The incoming tide
like a bowl of nickels.

We struggle and chime.

St. Andrew, you graygreen
spire. Gloucester Harbor,
splinter through the courtyard
gates. Sunflowers, candles.

5.

Vigorous and charming
the baseball hats and commemorative
coins of the bicentennial.
The rotting hulls of the last tall ships.

Daisystar, pulled by the plague
of storms and foglights,
sinking fast, amongst calls for

more rope.

I am some sad potatoes.
Which is also awful.

It is Monday, the same Monday
or another Monday come around,
and the petulant lights of the churchtop
warn off small planes

like a children's book lighthouse.

LOUPE

In bed at dusk. Through
the window a net of birds spreads
over the convex bay. Buildings
on the banks roll down through a screen

of light, and cracks show through the plaster:
a tamarack or the trestle of an elevated train.
The dress she wore
shades from pear to bruise

on a clothesline in the courtyard.
Watching light shift over the surface of water
gives way:
It is not myself I return to.

A bay has built its own reflection
with the symmetry of a graveyard.

AS, OR ISLE

Dress for me all in jersey,
the recluse of bedrooms, oceanliners,
prime-time television, as we would love
to love again the pigeons, to let the day burn
to a spindle of sun, its shorelines
all repetitions.

She has perfectly formed ears.
The general buffoonery of April
and the smell of fabric softener in the air.
We frail forward.
Comfort me lone to the cusp.

I, OR FAIRBORN

No one said we had to make our way alone.
Mid-day sun and codeine is Mount St. Helens.
Or when the sun gave out I don't mind to say
feeling awful, or say, go on.

Into bakelite evening erupting sideways,
but through windows: vagaries, ruined sight.
In a headlock, and we've bleached
our teeth with our tongues. The wish

to see them all: small, orderly, perfectly hatted
on the steps of the Museum of Natural History.
I will glow my eyes toward you dear St. Helens,
patron of loose change, spilt coffee, lost mail.

ONE MORE FOR THOMAS PAINE

may I be / your coterie?
—Anonymous

1.

When we lost your head,
I'm sorry.

I hear the cricket,
in the hole
in my tooth.

Night, and only the bakers
in their milk-light,

the newspaper trucks—
logoed,

eyes
full and breaking.

2.

Thick links of the river,
waves of gratitude,
semaphore swells.

Yardsale: one broken promise
after another.

Steamfit: what the hell
is the worst that can happen?

Star in the milkweed, year of the cavity,
antifreeze goes down smooth.

TAPS

A loss, having learned it,
opens to what is missed.

I feel better it is
Saturday pouring rain

in the season of scaffolds
and pharmaceuticals.

I get up at night to write down:
[illegible].

Now is the time for "Taps"
on the morning village green.

THE ONE IN WHICH THE SEAGULL
LAYS ITS HEAD BENEATH ITS WING

Dire is our footsteps
in the loom of December.

Heartspur, poison of the Teflon fire,
a blue like any other.

I'm asunder
with the plaints for your long lost button.

We lay, across the pharmacy counter
our broken strands of hair:

A boy, the shadow of a stone.
The stars awful in your head,
and in your mouth.

Gulls over the estuaries of Harlem,
how the cranes crane